Center
2836 S Chase Ave
Milw, WI 53207

414-446-7107

Messages from a Mother

The Love of my Life

by

Lacey Lafferty

authorHOUSE®

Contents

AuthorHouse™
1663 Liberty Drive
Bloomington, IN 47403
www.authorhouse.com
Phone: 1-800-839-8640

Published by AuthorHouse 10/16/12

ISBN: 978-1-4772-6823-0 (sc)
ISBN: 978-1-4772-6822-3 (hc)
ISBN: 978-1-4772-6821-6 (e)

Library of Congress Control Number: 2012917473

Messages from a Mother

Messages from a Mother have a purpose like non other, to show you the way, without troubling dismay,

Messages from a Mother help you along your way, to a future full of hope, heartache and happiness,

Messages from a Mother are there to protect you, from others that want to alarm you and harm you,

Messages from a Mother are meant to inspire you, to be the best you can be, educate yourself, where you can do their job, but they cannot do your job,

Messages from a Mother lead you down a path, that already has been traveled, not making the same mistakes that others made before you,

Messages from a Mother were not meant to suppress you, but up lift you, surpassing your potential, achieving goals leading to greatness, living your life, instead of life leaving you,

Messages from a Mother, gives you the feeling of a fond memory, a warm embrace, a presence watching over you and a Love that writes the message to You.

Chapter One

Lady

There periods in your life when you are
just being you, when an event is poignant,
allow the lady to emerge from oneself!

A good woman explains
herself, a great woman
explains nothing!

Be the woman, other
people wish they were!

A real woman is not afraid of getting her hands dirty; a great woman will not only get her your hands dirty, but encourage and educate others to do the same!

When you caught her in a lie, she is creatively coming up with another, to cover for that last one!

After a night out with my new boyfriend, I arrive home, my grandmother is waiting at the door, She's says, "It's after 11pm, I called his house and a woman answered the phone, who's she". I said, "Good question, I'll get back to you, after I choke on his words, that he wasn't involved with anyone".

Darling, please don't allow anyone to dictate your life, especially when you pay the bills!

Gals, just stroke his ego, he will follow you everywhere and believe you're the most wonderful person he has ever met!

Grace

I look in the mirror; I see my brown hair
with a slight of silver glair,

I look in the mirror; I see the surface of
my face showing wear all over the place,

I look in the mirror; I see my blue eyes,
not as bright as before,

I look in the mirror; I see my teeth, need
a touch of whitener before the winter,

I look in the mirror, I see I am gradually
aging, but I do not fear the final finale,

For I am happy with my face, now that I
look like my mother Grace!

I am the kind of woman who believes in what she wants, fights for what she gets, walks with my head held high, will not waiver when approached, have no excuses for my actions, I am strong, hear me roar, for I am near, oh no, she is here!

Your friends will come and go, but Mom and Dad have got your back and that's a fact, through thick and thin, to the end!

I never said I was perfect, I said I was good, I do and will make mistakes, but I am woman enough to admit them and correct them, I will not give up, but live up, to the image my child will be proud of!

If she cheated on her husband with you, she'll eventually move on, when another gets her groove on!

In measuring a woman's character,
She invokes instinctive dedication,
In preserving her children's wellbeing,
Instead of indulging selfish desires!

Chapter Two
Face Lift

To peel off life-long layers of emotions and drama, create a new you with good feelings and vibrations that enhance your quality of life!

There is nothing like the feeling, of being independent and in charge of your life, pursuing your goals and achieving greatness in whatever endeavor you have chosen!

Being happy means more than being desperate, improvise with a replacement that has a meaningful purpose!

If you can't win, be spectacular!

Biggest challenge you face is not what you see, it's your minds attempt to conquer the chosen task!

You may not like my life, but it's the life I chose, it fits my purpose, the purpose I have chosen!

If someone angers you, they have conquered you, be above it!

Courage lies in the heart, believe in yourself, stand up for what is right and display it like a lion.

The future is forever, never give up, time will tell, if it was meant to be yours, it will come to you!

Go with the flow, the river of life, will carry you to your destiny!

There is nothing more fulfilling and rewarding, then getting paid for doing a job you love to do, plan your life's career path, save for a rainy day and retirement, life can be easy, just make a plan and stick to it!

Fear nothing, fear no one, when fear erupts, challenge it, face it, conquer it, praise yourself, bask in the glow of glory!

My destiny is mine, allow no one to derail your dreams, allow nothing to stand in your way, do not accept failure as an option, pursue and accomplish your goal!

I don't want for anything; God gave me everything I need,
He gave me the knowledge and the know-how,
He gave me the guts, grit and the glory,
He gave me the drive and determination,
He gave me the muscle and the motivation,
He gave me the ability to fear no obstacles,
He gave me dreams, to pursue my destiny!

To be great, you have to believe you're the greatest, if not, pretend you are!

God gave you the will power, to accomplish any endeavor that your mind created!

You create your own happiness, no one else owes it to you, happiness is what you create and make of it!

Do something that makes another life better, for it is truly a humbling experience!

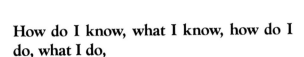

How do I know, what I know, how do I do, what I do,
God walks with me and he talks with me; God guides my hand, where I truly understand,
God gives me the people, the place and the things, to bring it all together,
It is up to me, to carefully craft my character into the person that knows what to do and how to do it!

I believe you better control your
attitude or it will control you,
I believe you better control your
behavior or it will control you,
Once you are in control, I
believe you can be as powerful
as the sun rising in the east and
resting in the west!

I don't want to hear "I can't do it", everyone can do it, put forth the effort, forge ahead through obstacles, achieve greatness, I faith in you!

Inspiration comes from your perseverance to achieve greatness, conquering your fears, striving for more instead of less!

I have an angel sitting on my shoulder, telling me to take it slower, shouting, "You are getting older",
Do not jog to fast or your legs will not last,
Save your back, anything could cause a heart attack,
Watch that look in your eyes, as your blood begins to rise,
It shows the flushness in your face, fickle flair of your flaming temper,
Cool yourself down, wipe that frown,
God's not ready for you to wear that crown,
Take your life slow and bask in the glow,
In time you will know, your life was worth the show!

If I were you and you were me, would you stand up or would you stand down, I for one would stand my ground!

Everyone deserves praise after a job well done, heightens awareness for the people around them.

You inspire me, when you
look at me
You inspire me, when you
hold my hand
You inspire me, when you hug
me tight
You inspire me, when you kiss
me goodnight
You inspire me, to be the best
I can be
You inspire me, for you and me!

It's nifty to be fifty, stuff everything in swiftly, run in the sun, swim in the surf, go away on adventures, be fun and festive, I'm gonna do it, come on and hold me to it, gonna fill that list and it's not just a gist, before it all ends, let's blend it all in, It's nifty to be fifty!

Live Life to be Me

I live life my own way, I stand up for
myself, my beliefs and those I love,

I speak my mind with my own thoughts
and do things my own way,

I am a leader and not a follower, my inner
strength will preserve over weakness,

I will not allow anyone to step on me,
overcome me or abuse me,

If I am challenged, I welcome it, I thrive
on it, it makes my life rewarding,

If I intimidate you with my presence,
except me for who and what I am,

What this means to me, is that I have
courage, strength, integrity and honor to
allow myself to be ME!

The word Love gets spoken easily, if it is
real, you will know it, your face will show
it and your body will glow it!

Life is too short, to sweat the small stuff,
chill out and start living it up!

After fifty, open a new chapter; wake up motivated, go after everything, leaving no stone unturned creates new goals, achieve greatness, inspire others, map out your destiny, and make a difference in your life, for the rest of your life!

Make education a passion, knowledge is power, learn anything and do everything, be marketable, in the long run, it will be you that can do their job, but they cannot do your job!

I deal with situations methodically and effectively, using my mind over the matter, at a competent level to achieve the end result!

Allow every day to become the best and most beautiful experience; live it like there is no tomorrow, throughout your life, with no regrets!

I am not ashamed of who I am, what I am, what I have done, where I came from or where I will go from here, my future is endless!

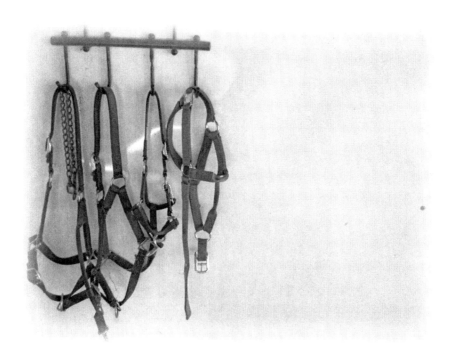

On the edge of desperation,
Around the corner of despair,
Over the crest of the hill of
disheartenment,
Tip of the iceberg in
depression,
Last straw of dejection,
When you are lost and
hopeless,
God says, "Believe in me
and I will help you believe in
yourself, for I will lead you
to the light of hope, love and
enlightenment".

Open your mind let the knowledge in,
Open your eyes let the light in,
Open your heart let the lord in!

God gave man, the will to persevere under
extreme pressures, to succeed above man's
own limitations.

I knew early in life, if I wanted anything, I had to apply myself above all others, strive to achieve greatness, conquer any fears, be the best I could be in everything I do, my goal is not to win everything, but be real good at everything!

Reflection is powerful, it can make you change the way you look at yourself and others!

Stand up for yourself and what you know is right, no one else will, respect your decision and people will respect you.

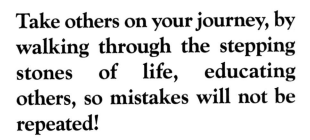

Take others on your journey, by walking through the stepping stones of life, educating others, so mistakes will not be repeated!

If a person is not willing to change, they are not worth waiting for, don't accept nothing but the best for yourself, because the best will only do!

Wisdom of my life will not deceive me, for I have gained a memory of knowledge, which will be with me forever!

Winners never quit, quitters never win, winning is wonderful!

Just remember this, you cannot go through a wall, you can go over, you can go under, you can go around, never give in, never give up, you improvise and you conquer, just remember, you work for it, it will be yours!

Believe me, you don't bother me, I won't let you!

You spot it, you got it, go get it!

Chapter Three
Endangering Youngster

Children look up to their peers for guidance with enthusiasm to gain knowledge that will form their personalities!

A question was presented to
my daughter,
"Who is your hero?"
She answered, "My Mommy"
Just affirms my belief, be the
best you can be, when no one
else notices, she did!

I picked up my daughter from school one afternoon and she joyfully stated, "Mom, me and the boys were catching caterpillars and crickets at recess today, that is awesome, I love my life". All I could think of was, at six years old, she already hanging with the boys, what am I going to do when she is sixteen!

One of the greatest feelings about having a child, I get to re-live my childhood all over again, creating lovely memories with my daughter!

Children come first, oneself comes second, everyone else, get a ticket and stand in line.

What most disturbs me, is crimes against children, a heartless human inflicts harm upon a giving soul, with the sole purpose to destroy its innocence!

Fear

I never knew what fear felt like, until I was faced with the decision, to give the life of my child to a doctor's scalpel, that could possibly end her life as we know it or enhance it into the next generation. It truly scared the hell out of me.

Mold the young mind with love and laughter, for it builds their character with endearing qualities, throughout their lifetime!

There is no other feeling, like the feeling you get, when a child wraps their arms around you and says, "I love you".

When parents neglect their children, mentally and physically, children seek guidance and compassion from others, some in growth and happiness, others in sorrow and sadness, they can be easily taken advantage and fall prey to predators!

You never know how much patience you have, until you have a child, love them, teach them, discipline them, evolving into a sensible and compassionate human being!

Give children praise when earned, encourage them to be the best they can be!

The sacrifices a mother makes for their child; keeping the peace within the family, hiatus from a career, others needs before their own, multi-tasking with everyday chores, creating more with less, try to earn a living while balancing child care and someone said this wasn't a job!

Take care of our children, whatever the cost or our future will be lost, educate them with real sense instead of nonsense, someday they will be in charge of our countries duties, when we become discharged from our country's needs, be kind to our youth, for they will feel the truth of our ways, to our endless days!

True Love

I feel fortunate to have known and felt true love, for I feel it, when I hold her close, for I see it, when I look into her eyes, the warmth that comes over me, when she speaks to me, I lien on her, she liens on me, we have a bond that cannot be broken, she is special to me, she was created with love by you and me!

When a child has surgery, you find just how precious a life can be, when the child is your own, how deep your love has grown, how you ever managed alone!

Chapter Four
Canyon Thoughts

Deep thinking, replenishes the body, mind and soul, towards aspirations that are enlightening!

A mind is like an umbrella, it's not going to work, unless it's open and for some, it needs to be left open!

Be careful of sneaky people, they hold secrets, think they are smarter, but actually dumber, trying to impress, only to regress, deep down there inferior, truly a non-believer!

How can anyone choose a desire of the flesh or another's advances over their own child's physical and mental wellbeing! It just boggles the mind!

People will judge you on first impressions and visual observations, keep yourself and your house clean, a thing for every place, a place for everything, cleanliness is next to Godliness!

If a person has enough compassion to offer their resources, whether physical or financial, without being asked, it measures the depth of their heart!

When your body controls your mind, desire takes over sense, body succumbs to pleasure, hope you made your choice wisely!

When the telephone keeps ringing, with a familiar number and you won't answer it, one would have to assume, someone doesn't want to talk, how a brain ceases to function when emotions cloud its judgments!

Don't burn bridges; you might need to cross it, on the road, into your future!

The people God gave you, love them dearly, one day God will call them back home!

God gave me my brain, don't test my intelligence and insult his craftsmanship!

Every action creates a reaction, so does success and failure!

Falling in lust, is not falling in love, don't go too fast, for it won't last, get to know them, then show them, don't attempt to mold them into a fantasy image of your knight in shining armor, only to have a retard in tin foil, love them or leave them!

In adolescence, the fear of getting pregnant, shaming oneself and their family, was more powerful, then allowing a moment of lust to influence ones decision, preservation of one's honor and integrity was more important!

When you have entered the second phase of life, you like to be wined and dined, dazzled with diamonds, along with the finer things of life.
Don't stress on anything less!

I have seen the life leave the body of a friend, before their last breath, only to say, "I see the light", never to say hello or goodbye, never to return, to lie eternity in an urn, a forever friend to the end!

People will accept you for your generous spirit, before your intellectual ideas!

I am always going to be there for you, every breath I make, every step I take, every decision you choose, I will not let you fail, whether in body or in spirit, I will be there for you!

I am with you

When they lay me down, do not cry, I am with you,
Even though I took my last breath, I am with you,
Even though my skin lost its pinkish glow, I am with you,
Even though you don't hear my voice, I am with you,
Even though when shaken, no movement awaken, I am with you,
For I am resting in a peaceful place with the people we love, know that I love you,
We are with you!

Don't miss a moment, by sleeping your life
away, you sleep all you want, when you die
and you are laid to rest!

Laugh and the world laughs with you, cry
and you cry alone, that will happen a lot
when you're married!

When a person says, they love you, watch the behavior reflect the word that is spoken, if it doesn't match, it isn't genuine, take the time to know someone, before you take that leap of faith!

Educate oneself with life experiences, with wisdom, knowledge and faith, it will help you handle decisions and disappoints, will enable you to persevere well into your golden years!

I might not do everything the lord wants me too, but when I need him, I call him and he is there!

For those who often think that some jobs are such an inconvenience, making excuses does not justify not doing the job that needs to be done, when in fact, the job that needs to be done is more important than the job that was easier!

A true and lasting relationship is when you tell each other anything and everything, no secrets, no lies, just be real with each other and you both will grow old together!

Every day, ordinary people are doing extra ordinary things for perfect strangers that embody the American spirit!

¶ am an American;

I am a descendent from one of America's founding Fathers of the Declaration of Independence, ninth generation granddaughter of John Morton.

I am proud of the heritage he left for all Americans, for he sacrificed himself for all of us to enjoy our freedom and the liberty to express ourselves!

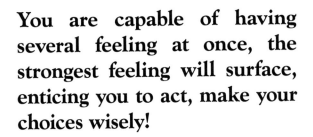

You are capable of having several feeling at once, the strongest feeling will surface, enticing you to act, make your choices wisely!

Truly, I cannot believe government is so helplessly politically driven, that the minds of men and women can be deluded with trivial nonsense, when children derive with a better solutions through logical understanding, there is still hope.

Take some moments for yourself, close your eyes, clear your mind, take a breath, reflect and direct, where you want your energy to flow, if you can't feel it, allow the pen to compose it, then the mind will perceive it!

The Lord gives us the strength to solve our own problems with the intelligence to create solutions.

The second phases of life, create a bucket list, do something new, and make your life exciting!

The mind is truly surprising, when out of desperation, people, animals and insects can adapt to circumstances, inspire themselves, creative, imaginative and clever in building the foundation for their dreams!

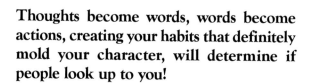

Thoughts become words, words become actions, creating your habits that definitely mold your character, will determine if people look up to you!

To see the sunrise in the morning,
To feel the splendor of the day beginning,
To see the clouds above,
To feel the softness of the light shining through,
To see the sunset in the evening,
To feel the warmth of the world around you!

It will only last forever, if there is trust in the beginning, in the middle and in the end!

Never apologize for stating what you believe, that's like stating you're sorry for being honest!

Wanted by many, taken by none, looking at some, waiting for one!

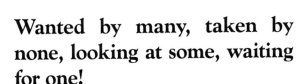

Unlock your fears and your world will open to unlimited triumphs!

Warm embrace,
Leads to a hot kiss,
Erupts into a wild mess,

Results in a sleep-full bliss!

Instead of spending your time trying to find out what wrong with everything, happiness is finding out what right with everything!

Who they are and what they do must matter first to themselves, then the good of who they are with, in order to love, they must first love themselves!

Once you have achieved who you are, only then can you espier others!

His Morning Touch

He woke me this morning with a slight
touch of his hand,

I lay there thinking, hoping this day will
be grand,

I sprang to my feet, with a stretch and a
yawn,

Peeping out the window to discover it's
barely dawn,

He pushed me through the house with his
vim and vigor,

Enough to say, there's a lot of work today,
get it together,

As I stepped out the door and into the
morning light,

I thanked him, for it's a glorious sight,

Through the day, he is in my thoughts,

I say to myself, please give me the strength,
the courage,

To accomplish his task, in case he asks,

As I lay my head down, my body outright
this night,

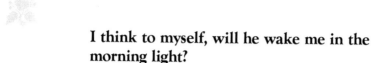

I think to myself, will he wake me in the morning light?

I guess my question, he only knows,

If I awake with the shake of his elbows,

Before my eyes close, one last thing I would like to say as I doze,

Thank you for giving me the time to see, hear, smell, touch

The splendor of your world and of course, your universe,

When my job is done, for you will know,

I will not wake with a shake, because he has called me home,

For he is God, he is The Lord, he will decide when my job is done,

Here on our earthly kingdom.

Chapter Five

Innocents of Animals

When you look into their eyes, they are looking into yours, searching for each other's souls, empathy and compassion for the living!

Animals look up at you with their soulful eyes, in hope that you will take care of them, until they take their old age last breath, in return they give you unconditional love that brings joy and laughter to your life!

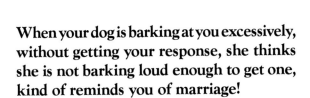

When your dog is barking at you excessively, without getting your response, she thinks she is not barking loud enough to get one, kind of reminds you of marriage!

There is got to be horses in heaven, be a lonely place, without such grace, cannot stand the thought, please I would be so distraught, it's been a long walk from here to there, hoping I will meet a horse at our Father's heavenly estate before it's too late, spending eternity couldn't be nicer then with Gods horse, Dancer!

The passion in my life is horses; they bring such pleasure, playfulness and delight, to my days that have turned into decades of everlasting joy!

One of my friends is my dog, I can talk all I want, how loud I want, as long as I want and she's happy to hear it!

Heaven is going to be a lonely place, if there are no horses!

I look at my horse, he looks at me, with those big steely eyes, thinking with a warm glee, I move towards him with ease, enough to say please, can I rub your warm nose, for a moment geez, he extends his muzzle to meet my mitten, rest assured I am smitten!

You know when your best friend is an animal; it is when you can openly discuss issues, without wanting to hear an insightful response.

An industry that is obligated to protect the sport of kings allows abuses by the hand of man, for profit and glory, is at best a sport that cannot police themselves, should be abolished, for God will punish all those that destroy his noble steads!

Chapter Six
Duke

Growing up with an image of a good man, a strong man, a man that takes care of business without creating difficulty, hard feelings and bad relationships with others!

If you discover your man is cheating on you, there is plenty of blame to go around, don't put all the blame on the other woman, put all the blame on your man, if he lied to you; you know he lied to her too!

Guys take time to be with her or someone else will make the time!

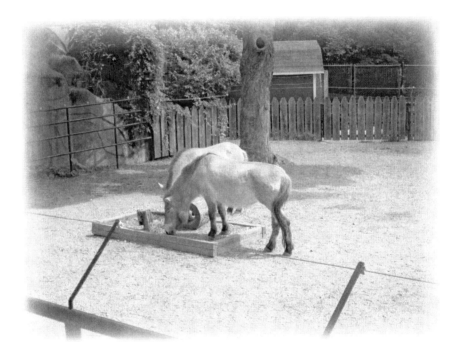

A good man listens to her story; a great man offers to help!

Don't expect me to give myself to you, when your committed to another, man up, make a choice!

If he cheated on his wife with you, he will cheat on you, with another and another and another!

In measuring a man's character,
He volunteers his parental responsibilities,
Instead of being summoned!

Real women can wear men's clothes and still keep their feminine flair; great women can wear anything to keep a gentlemen's stare!

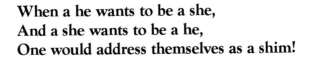

When a he wants to be a she,
And a she wants to be a he,
One would address themselves as a shim!

Staying single for the perfect man or woman, if they exist, if not, at least your happy, instead of miserable with a replacement!

If a man has to be told to bring it to your table of life, he wasn't worth the entree.

When you caught him in a lie, he has a lot more stored where that that one came from!

Have you ever watched a cat, oh boy, can they scat, got to watch them claws, just like your in-laws, they go creeping around, just like men sneaking abound, they think their slick, a man and his trick, watch those eyes, for they will lie, they run hard and fast, but in the end men are always last!

Our society needs to teach our daughters to distinguish between:

Men who flatter her and a men who compliment her, Men who spend money on her and a men who invest in her,

Men who view her as property and a men who view her properly,

Men who lust after her and a men who love her,

Men who believe he is a gift to women and men, who believes she is a gift to him,

And then our society needs to teach our sons to be that kind of men!

Chapter Seven

Tighten my Jaw

When you feel your teeth clenched, your jaw aching from the tension, your brow impeding your sight, the heat of your blood rising to your head, someone better

beware!

A lie always returns home, may not be today, may not be tomorrow, may not be next week or next year, but eventually a lie will not die, it will surface with a vengeance, only to destroy dreams and wreck relationships!

Life is short, to waste minute on anyone or anything that takes away precious moments of happiness, is just absurd!

If you have to say the same things over and over, obviously your either alone among many or many aren't worth your company.

Never say never, just when you do, fate is going to take a big bite right out of your ass!

Be nice, get nice things!

There are those that make repeated comments, bragging about themselves among others, it is ones attempt to justify their inadequacies, low self-esteem and their behavior is not appealing, if one is happy with themselves and their accomplishments, bragging is not necessary!

If the break up is painful, have some dignity and continue on with your life, with a lesson learned and your head held high, you might salvage a long lasting friendship instead!

Character is a carefully crafted mold of one's personal being, that results in good or bad behavior!

At fifty, I've seen it all, I've heard it all, and I've done it all, I just can't remember it all!

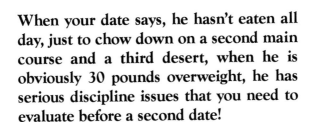

When your date says, he hasn't eaten all day, just to chow down on a second main course and a third desert, when he is obviously 30 pounds overweight, he has serious discipline issues that you need to evaluate before a second date!

When a conversation becomes heated, please remain seated, tempers will flair, you should care, behave yourself with dignity, for there are some, that need to read George Washington's book on Civility!

Don't marry an imperfect partner, even
if they shower you with gold, money and
diamonds, keep it simple in case you want
a quick exit!

There are moments when someone speaks with such disdain for anything and everything around themselves, a thousand miles away would not be far enough from such a person!

Don't create drama, where there is none,

keep it simple!

If you are looking for someone to beg you
to stay, that someone does not live here!

Don't put it off till tomorrow,
what you can do today, tomorrow
has enough to do!

Never say, "Never"
I will fight forever and ever!
Till the earth and moon come
together!

People tend to put on a good act, when creating first impressions, eventually their behavior will emerge to the surface, cracks in their armor will appear, determining whether they are truly genuine or toxic!

When someone comes into your life, destiny brought you together, for a reason, if it was meant to be, accept it, if not, get the hell out of Dodge!

A person has a long on and off relationship with another for 34 years, resulting in the bearing of a child, only to discover through admission, they are committed to another. Through their deceptive behavior, guarding oneself from the stories of lies forever!

Handling events with efficiency and discipline, quickly correct problems before they spin out of control, lasting effects lead to a more tranquil life here on earth!

Hate is a wasted emotion, get even, it feels better!

There is not a woman alive, that hasn't faked it!.

Be open to suggestions, hear one out, doesn't mean you have to do it, just means you are open minded and willing to listen to complaints, compliments and criticism!

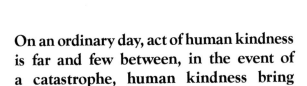

On an ordinary day, act of human kindness is far and few between, in the event of a catastrophe, human kindness bring together strangers!

Who do they think there messing with, they obviously don't know who they're messing with, it all stops here, and I am corporate!

I wish I may,
I wish I might,
I wish my dreams,
Come true tonight!

When you observe someone having problems in their life, that they could have easily thought through, the only thing comes to mind is, "Is that way working for you now", if not, you have to sit back, slow down, think things through with the Common Sense God gave you!

The good book says to forgive, but it is hard to forgive, when you let your guard down, allowing someone into your heart, only to discover they have lied to you, through manipulation and deception, you forever stay jaded!

Jealousy has several different faces, when one face raises its ugly head, it is you that can do his job, and it's he that cannot do your job, take that slap in the face!

What's unique about you, you're just as
unique as the universe, as the rivers, as the
mountains, as the shores, just as unique
as you!

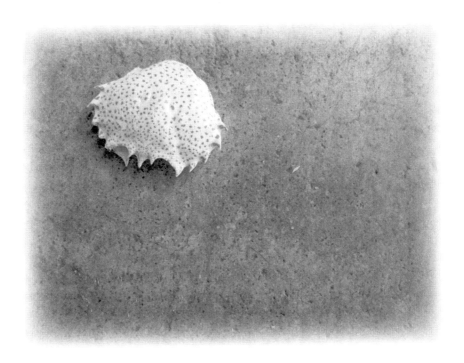

Just pluck another lie from the dusty storage shelf in a dark corner of one's brain, it destroys credibility and fools no one but oneself!

Keep yourself sane, live it, believe it, write it, tell it and if it feels right, flaught it!

One's jealousy is their own sense of insecurity with themselves, not with others!

Live every moment, like it's your last, you never know when you are going to run out of moments!

Cheating on a significant other only signified a personal conflict with their own morals!

Live every day, like it's your last, someday it will be!

When your significant other walks out of their home with another person and your only question is, "Are you doing something you shouldn't". Their response is, "Not now". Leave with some dignity and move on, because they obviously have!

I can have my cake and eat it too,
Because it's my party!

People, it's just another day, stop
the drama, have faith, it will all
come out in the wash!

Never believe what you hear, half what you see, behavior never lies!

My seventh sense just told me, he's full of it!

Nowhere does it say, you have to be faithful to an unfaithful lover, you are not committed, there is no union, no agreement, no ring on left finger, until the ink is dry!

Life is like the seasons, first 25 years
you spring into action, next 25 years you
summarize what your purpose is, following
25 years you fall into disrepair entering
your Golden Years, last 25 years your too
old and cold to care!

Once a liar, always a liar, it's speak volumes, especially when one has been in up-teen relationships simultaneously and married multiple times!

When you cross a path with a person, who made an unfavorable decision, that left a lasting bitter impression on your life, but decades later, you had the advantage of returning the favor, in a more profound way, just re-enforces the saying, what goes around, comes around. Patience is a virtue!

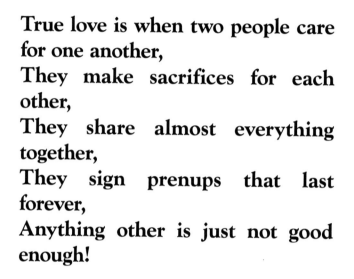

True love is when two people care for one another,
They make sacrifices for each other,
They share almost everything together,
They sign prenups that last forever,
Anything other is just not good enough!

If you like it,
Put a ring on it,
Otherwise don't complain about it,
When you neglect it,
And someone else does it!

What you see, what you hear, what you understand, make it your own, quote a life experience!

Some people will push your button's, your ability to set standards will keep them away!

Just when you thought, who else will say
something stupid today, a voice will say, "
I guess it's going to rain today", when it's
been raining all day!

I know some days can be real
rough and terribly tough, but
don't wish your life away, enjoy
your life today, tomorrow just
has to be better!

Don't feel sorry for them, they reap what they sow, when they were old enough to grow, they're old enough to know, what the consequences are to show!

During my first fifty years, I have found an excellent remedy for marriage;
Both parties have careers,
Both parties have separate bank accounts; Shared expenses come out of a shared bank account,
Child care is shared,
Both parties file separate tax returns,
Both parties keep their names to protect their identities,
Both parties get a prenup,
So when you are in the 50 percent that fails in marriage nothing is damaged other than your pride!

Sometimes your knight in shining armor
is just a retard in tin foil!

I don't care what you say; revenge is so,
too sweet!

Even though divulging secrets makes ones soul relieved, there are some events, one has to take to their grave, exposing would create too much pain for the living!

When someone shows anger first thing in the morning, one would presume that somebody fell off the wrong side of the bed, coffee pot didn't work, frosty flakes box was empty and the significant other didn't put the hopper seat down, the hair brush had doll hair in it, got a ticket on the way to work, show some compassion for the working Mom!

You thought you were too old
for surprises; when,
Your new boyfriend invites you
over his house, after you get off
of work, at midnight for your
birthday,
But he had to leave for a
moment, to run an errand,
As you sit there,
You hear the front door open
and the alarm turned off,
But you know that is not your
boyfriend, too soon,
Nervously you spring to your
feet,
Only to meet his ex-girlfriend
in the dark and you thought you
were too old for surprises!

When you find yourself lost in a relation-ship, it is time to squirrel money away for a rainy day - the day of independence, a business venture, a future endeavor!

When old flames have stabbed you in the back in the past, time does not change them; they will stab you in the back as long as you let them!

Person that steals is a cheating rat bastard,
with no morals, integrity or character!

Stupid is, what stupid does, just cannot
hide stupid!

Some people measure wealth with surrounding themselves with stuff, real wealth is the relationships you forge with others.

Somebody done somebody, somehow, somewhere, some say!

Stupid idiots are not born; they were made from mindless morons that poisoned the young minds of children, who were innocent at birth!

People that don't like surprises, are people that want to control everything and everybody!

If you rain on my parade, I'll trip your train!

If you expect something at my table of
life, you better bring something worthy,
at fifty, I don't work for free!

Tell them what they want to hear, it leads to the means, in what you want to achieve!

There is nothing I have done that I regret, only to have tweaked some things a little differently!

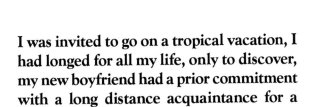

I was invited to go on a tropical vacation, I had longed for all my life, only to discover, my new boyfriend had a prior commitment with a long distance acquaintance for a weekend excursion.
Forget feelings, I am going on the trip!

A husband was seen talking and handing money to a women who drove unto the same area that she had propositioned herself the week earlier, when questioned he states, "She's lost and needed directions". Trust that builds a union is now forever broken as well as the marriage!

True relationships are based on;
Two hearts beating,
Two hands holding,
Two minds meeting,
Two souls greeting,
Two bodies blending,
And two to act as one!

When you walk the walk and talk the talk, are you prepared to back it up, only then will people take you seriously!

It is up to you, to find the beauty in the
ugliest of the universe around you!

Weak minded people, only have one track brains, the track that runs overboard!

What goes around, comes around, stays around, karma bites you all the way around!

Never say never, just when you thought you have heard it all, someone will approach you, with their unconventional wisdom, that leaves you with, "What the !!!!

Simple pleasures in life can be your favorite spaghetti dinner with wine, until you have eaten your first bite, only to discover, its wheat pasta!

Tell people what they want to hear;
Right, wrong or indifferent, they will
think you're the greatest thing since white
bread!

You got to ask yourself, if another is not contributing spiritually, physically, mentally and financially, kick them to the curb and look for another!

Sometimes you got to do, what you got to do, to get the job done, sometimes you're going to make people mad, but they're just going to have to get glad!

You live by the sword, you die by the sword, and no words have never ever better been spoken, live by them!

Memories from a Mother

Memories from a Mother is a bond we have together, no one can match what was made in heaven,

From birth to earth, through sickness and sadness,

From heartache to happiness, through joy and jubilation,

We laugh and we cry, for the time fly's by, we are getting older by the day, it is sad to say,

The memories we have made, pleasant places we have stayed,

Interesting people we greet, some are nice and really neat,

Activities we have conquered, through thick and thin, from beginning to end,

I learn from you and you learn from me and sometimes we even agree,

The memories I hold dear, are the words spoken I love you, so everyone can hear,

You are a part of me that only a Mother can see, from the first movement within me to the breath you make beside me,

I would lay down my life, if it meant saving your life, someday you will see, you are all that matters to me,

Some people have to be shown, when you have your own, how deep your love has grown,

We think about each other, even though were not together, our minds will meet whenever,

Memories from a Mother, is love non-other, it will last forever and ever.

Author Lacey lafferty retired Delaware State Trooper, model, agricultural business woman, a native of Lewes, now resides in Laurel, Delaware with her 7 year old daughter Lacey Lynn. Lacey received during her rewarding career in the Delaware State Police an Excellence Performance Award from Governor Minner in 2007. When faced with a life threatening illness in 2009, the thought of leaving her daughter without a mother's insight of life's everyday challenges, inspired Lacey to write Messages from a Mother. Messages from a Mother are Lacey's own personal experiences and reflections of her life through simple messages. These inspirational messages are meant to strengthen and encourage the reader to excel through adversity. In life there is no fool proof plan; access, evaluate and overcome.

CPSIA information can be obtained at www.ICGtesting.com
Printed in the USA
LVOW040455201112

307985LV00001B/5/P